30
Days

with

Augustine

a prayer book

Richard E. Buckner

BEACON HILL PRESS
OF KANSAS CITY

Library of Congress Cataloging-in-Publication
Buckner, Richard, 1961-
    30 Days with Augustine : a prayer book / Richard E. Buckner.
        pages cm
    Includes bibliographical references.
    ISBN 978-0-8341-3243-6 (flex cover)
    1. Devotional literature. I. Augustine, Saint, Bishop of Hippo. Works. Selections. English. II. Title.
III. Title: Thirty days with Augustine.
    BV4801.B77 2014
    242'.2—dc23

                                                                                              2014002712

10 9 8 7 6 5 4 3 2 1

Contents

The Lord's Prayer*

Our Father in heaven,
hallowed be your Name,
your kingdom come,
your will be done,
on earth as in heaven.
Give us today our daily bread.
Forgive us our sins
as we forgive those
who sin against us.
Save us from the time of trial,
and deliver us from evil.
For the kingdom, the power,
and the glory are yours,
now and forever. Amen.

*BCP

"Take Up and Read"

Turning points in life sometimes happen in the most unexpected ways. An ordinary event can kindle to full blaze what for so long was only a flicker. An innocent phrase by a child can take on life-changing consequences. For Augustine, the words "take up and read" had this very effect.

Struggling with whether he could truly embrace the Christian lifestyle, this future bishop and theologian, on hearing a child say these words, took up a book of Scripture lying nearby and read from it. It was a passage from the book of Romans.[1] Suddenly he felt a release from his inner conflict. While reading, he had received the spiritual strength he needed to become the man of faith he longed to be.[2]

Born in AD 354 in Tagaste, North Africa, this brilliant thinker and defender of the faith was reared by his saintly mother, Monica, who unceasingly prayed for him and saw to his education in the Christian faith. Yet Augustine's intellectual wanderlust carried him from the dualism of Manichaeism to the spiritual leanings of Neoplatonism. This philosophical pursuit combined with his self-indulgent lifestyle, his prestige as an exceptional teacher, and assorted personal misgivings delayed his taking up the cross of Christ. But despite these hindrances God intersected his life. His mother's prayers, the influence of friends and acquaintances, and his own reflections prepared the way for what happened when he responded to the child's voice in AD 386.

From this point on, Augustine's life changed dramatically. After he was baptized, he sold his property and gave the proceeds to the poor, took up a life of prayer and meditation, and eventually became a priest and later a bishop. He became famous for his teaching and astute reasoning, and he

---

1. Augustine read from Rom. 13:13-14.
2. Justo González's account (*A History of Christian Thought*, 2nd ed. [Nashville: Abingdon Press, 1987]) was especially helpful in clarifying that Augustine received at this time the "power" to live the Christian life to which he had already "intellectually converted" (24).

defended the Christian faith with great depth and ability. From his autobiographical *Confessions* to his vision of history in *The City of God*, along with theological treatises, sermons, and numerous works defending the church against its opponents,[3] Augustine wielded a formidable pen. His thinking, writing, and service to Christ's church have stood the test of time, with his influence reaching to the present day—and all because God met him at an opportune moment and remade his life.

Like Augustine's story, the major crossroads in our lives are at first glance often just simple events, routine encounters with people, and commonplace gestures. When combined with prayer, what is ordinary often becomes extraordinary as we see more clearly the working of God's grace, and then our lives are drawn in a new direction, one we may have never considered before. Prayer itself is thus a setting and an occasion where the chance that life may change its course is perhaps the greatest. Not surprisingly, Augustine was in the throes of prayer when he heard the child's voice.

30 Days with Augustine is a book of prayer and hence a reservoir of possibilities—opportunities to regularly experience the life-changing effects of God's presence. Designed to mirror the order of traditional Christian prayer, each day is divided into morning and evening devotional times. Morning sections combine psalms, hymns, and prayers with selections from the writings of Augustine. Evening sections, although similar to the morning sections, are shorter and also include self-examination questions to promote spiritual growth. Each day ends with space to record personal thoughts and insights. Taken together, the different features provide a setting for worship and transformation, along with valuable reflections from one of Christendom's greatest minds.

As with most prayer books, this one may be used by individuals or groups. Traditionally, prayer books served to unite the prayers of a community. Whether gathered in one place or separated by distance, believers could join together in spirit by praying the appointed prayers assigned to specific times of the day. Drawing small groups and congregations together through this practice can be one of the most valuable uses of a prayer book.

---

3. Augustine met the challenges of groups such as the Manichaeans, Donatists, and Pelagians.

For some believers, praying psalms and written prayers may be an unfamiliar practice, but it is not intended to replace praying spontaneously. Each devotional section of this book includes a time for offering private intercessions and praises. The prayers, hymns, psalms, and reflections function as guides to deepen and widen the scope of personal prayer.

Many of the hymns and selections from the writings of Augustine have been adapted to contemporary standards of grammar and style. Where possible, pronouns such as "thee" and "thy" have been replaced with "you" and "your," phrases have been updated, and punctuation has been revised. The prayers themselves are designed to complement the other components, and the accountability questions are based on biblical admonitions such as those in the Ten Commandments and the epistles of Paul.

Augustine, bishop of Hippo, died in AD 430 having made the most of a redeemed and transformed life. God had met him when he was ready to embrace a new way of living, and he responded wholeheartedly. God had used other people and circumstances—even the playful words of a child—to prepare Augustine for that moment; it was a turning point saturated in God's grace. May this prayer book help those who use it find and respond to those moments of decision God has in store for them. To echo the words that Augustine heard so long ago, "Take up, read . . . and pray!"

DAY 1 † Morning Prayer

O Lord, open my lips, and my mouth will declare your praise. (Ps. 51:15, NRSV)

Psalm 95:1-2

Come, let us sing for joy to the LORD;
    let us shout aloud to the Rock of our salvation.
Let us come before him with thanksgiving
    and extol him with music and song.

Glory to the Father, and to the Son, and to the Holy Spirit: as it was in the beginning, is now, and will be forever. Amen.

Hymn

Stand up and bless the Lord;
    The Lord your God adore.
Stand up and bless his glorious name
    Now and forevermore.

Psalm 146:1-2, 6

Praise the LORD.
Praise the LORD, my soul.
I will praise the LORD all my life;
    I will sing praise to my God as long as I live.

. . . .

He is the Maker of heaven and earth,
    the sea, and everything in them—
    he remains faithful forever.

Prayer

O Lord, we bless your holy name, for you have made the entire universe and care for its every part—the stars, the land, the sea, and all living things.

Psalm 147:1-5

Praise the LORD.
How good it is to sing praises to our God,
    how pleasant and fitting to praise him!
The LORD builds up Jerusalem;
    he gathers the exiles of Israel.
He heals the brokenhearted
    and binds up their wounds.
He determines the number of the stars
    and calls them each by name.
Great is our Lord and mighty in power;
    his understanding has no limit.

Prayer

We offer to you, O God, pleasant praise for gathering us together into a people redeemed by the blood of your Son and for healing our hearts bruised by sin.

Scripture Reading (Optional) Hebrews 13:15

Reflections from Augustine

Great are you, O Lord, and greatly to be praised; great is your power, and of your wisdom there is no end. And we, being a part of your creation, desire to praise you—we who carry around with us our mortality, the witness of our sin, even the witness that you "resist the proud"—yet we, as part of your creation, desire to praise you. You move us to delight in praising you, for you have formed us for yourself, and our hearts are restless till they find rest in you. (*Confessions*, 1.1.1)

(Offer personal prayers.)

The Lord's Prayer

Dismissal

Draw closely to us today, O Father. Help us to glorify you in all we do. This we ask through Christ Jesus, our Lord. Amen.

DAY 1 † Evening Prayer

Self-Examination

(Reflect on the day, using the following questions as a guide, confess any departures from the law of love, and ask God for forgiveness.)

- Have I today loved and honored God before everything else in my life?
- Have I been kind and compassionate to my coworkers, friends, and family?

Opening

O God, come to my assistance; O Lord, make haste to help me.
(Ps. 69:2, DRA)*

Glory to the Father, and to the Son, and to the Holy Spirit: as it was in the beginning, is now, and will be forever. Amen.

Luke 1:46-49

My soul glorifies the Lord
   and my spirit rejoices in God my Savior,
for he has been mindful
   of the humble state of his servant.
From now on all generations will call me blessed,
   for the Mighty One has done great things for me—
   holy is his name.

Intercessions

(Offer personal prayers.)

Lord's Prayer

Dismissal

Grant us peace and rest, O God, so that refreshed, we may awaken to love and serve you, through Christ Jesus, our Lord. Amen.

*Psalm 70:1 in most modern versions of the Bible.

Personal Meditations

DAY 2 † Morning Prayer

O Lord, open my lips, and my mouth will declare your praise. (Ps. 51:15, NRSV)

Psalm 95:6-7

Come, let us bow down in worship,
    let us kneel before the LORD our Maker;
for he is our God
    and we are the people of his pasture,
    the flock under his care.

Glory to the Father, and to the Son, and to the Holy Spirit: as it was in the beginning, is now, and will be forever. Amen.

Hymn

Come, thou Fount of every blessing,
    Tune my heart to sing thy grace.
Streams of mercy, never ceasing,
    Call for songs of loudest praise.

Psalm 1:1-3

Blessed is the one
    who does not walk in step with the wicked
or stand in the way that sinners take
    or sit in the company of mockers,
but whose delight is in the law of the LORD,
    and who meditates on his law day and night.
That person is like a tree planted by streams of water,
    which yields its fruit in season
and whose leaf does not wither—
    whatever they do prospers.

Prayer

O Heavenly Father, keep our hearts centered on your Son, the Living Word, through whom we find sustenance to flourish like trees rooted deeply beside flowing waters.

Psalm 3:1-4

LORD, how many are my foes!
>How many rise up against me!
Many are saying of me,
>"God will not deliver him."
But you, LORD, are a shield around me,
>my glory, the One who lifts my head high.
I call out to the LORD,
>and he answers me from his holy mountain.

Prayer

We thank you, O Lord, for hearing us when we call to you amid our many cares and for upholding us with the comforting strength of your Holy Spirit.

Scripture Reading (Optional)   Hebrews 12:1-13

Reflections from Augustine

Hear my prayer, O Lord. Do not let me become discouraged under your discipline, nor let me grow weary in acknowledging your mercies through which you have saved me from all my sinful ways. These things I ask of you so that you might become sweeter to me than all that used to entice me, that I may love you entirely and grasp your hand with my whole heart, and that you may deliver me from every temptation, even to the end. (*Confessions*, 1.15.24)

(Offer personal prayers.)

The Lord's Prayer

Dismissal

May our lives so reflect your love, O God, that others may be graced with a glimpse of you. This we pray in the name of your Son, Christ Jesus, our Lord. Amen.

DAY 2 † Evening Prayer

Self-Examination

(Reflect on the day, using the following questions as a guide, confess any departures from the law of love, and ask God for forgiveness.)

- Have I held a vision of God's love and mercy that is narrow and exclusive?
- Has a limited vision of God harmed my relationships with others?

Opening

O God, come to my assistance; O Lord, make haste to help me.
(Ps. 69:2, DRA)

Glory to the Father, and to the Son, and to the Holy Spirit: as it was in the beginning, is now, and will be forever. Amen.

Luke 1:50-51

[The Lord's] mercy extends to those who fear him,
    from generation to generation.
He has performed mighty deeds with his arm;
    he has scattered those who are proud in
their inmost thoughts.

Intercessions

(Offer personal prayers.)

Lord's Prayer

Dismissal

As we take our slumber, O God, surround us through the night with your soothing and protective love. In the name of Christ, we pray. Amen.

Personal Meditations

DAY 3 † Morning Prayer

O Lord, open my lips, and my mouth will declare your praise. (Ps. 51:15, NRSV)

Psalm 100:1-2

Shout for joy to the LORD, all the earth.
Worship the LORD with gladness;
come before him with joyful songs.

Glory to the Father, and to the Son, and to the Holy Spirit: as it was in the beginning, is now, and will be forever. Amen.

Hymn

The Lord is never far away,
But through all grief distressing,
An ever-present help and stay,
Our peace and joy and blessing.

Psalm 6:2-4

Have mercy on me, LORD, for I am faint;
heal me, LORD, for my bones are in agony.
My soul is in deep anguish.
How long, LORD, how long?
Turn, LORD, and deliver me;
save me because of your unfailing love.

Prayer

We thank you, O Lord, for hearing us in our brokenness and for soothing our care-worn souls with the comforting presence of your Holy Spirit.

Psalm 10:12-14, 17-18

Arise, LORD! Lift up your hand, O God.
Do not forget the helpless.
Why does the wicked man revile God?
Why does he say to himself,
"He won't call me to account"?

16

But you, God, see the trouble of the afflicted;
>   you consider their grief and take it in hand.
The victims commit themselves to you;
>   you are the helper of the fatherless.

. . . .

You, LORD, hear the desire of the afflicted;
>   you encourage them, and you listen to their cry,
defending the fatherless and the oppressed,
>   so that mere earthly mortals
>   will never again strike terror.

Prayer

Father in heaven, we praise you, for even when you seem far away, you are close at hand and always faithful. Through the victory of your Son, Jesus, justice has dawned for the helpless and needy.

Scripture Reading (Optional)   Matthew 5:43-48

Reflections from Augustine

It is a smaller thing to wish well or even to do good to people who have done no evil to you. It is a much higher thing—an act of supreme goodness—to love your enemies and always to wish well and seek to do good to the people who wish you ill and desire to do you harm. This is to obey the command of God: "Love your enemies, do good to them who hate you, and pray for them who persecute you." (*Enchiridion*, chap. 73)

(Offer personal prayers.)

The Lord's Prayer

Dismissal

Strengthen us with your Holy Spirit, O Father, so that we may meet the challenges of the day while obeying your command to love, through Christ Jesus, our Lord. Amen.

DAY 3 † Evening Prayer

Self-Examination

(Reflect on the day, using the following questions as a guide, confess any departures from the law of love, and ask God for forgiveness.)

- Have my words about God or my use of his name failed to properly represent his holiness and love?
- Has my behavior hindered others from desiring to know and praise God?

Opening

O God, come to my assistance; O Lord, make haste to help me.
(Ps. 69:2, DRA)

Glory to the Father, and to the Son, and to the Holy Spirit: as it was in the beginning, is now, and will be forever. Amen.

Luke 1:52-53

[The Lord] has brought down rulers from their thrones
    but has lifted up the humble.
He has filled the hungry with good things
    but has sent the rich away empty.

Intercessions

(Offer personal prayers.)

Lord's Prayer

Dismissal

Restore us, good Lord, as we sleep so that we may greet the morning invigorated for an abundance of good works to the honor and glory of your name, in which we pray. Amen.

Personal Meditations

DAY 4 † Morning Prayer

O Lord, open my lips, and my mouth will declare your praise. (Ps. 51:15, NRSV)

Psalm 100:3

Know that the LORD is God.
  It is he who made us, and we are his;
  we are his people, the sheep of his pasture.

Glory to the Father, and to the Son, and to the Holy Spirit: as it was in the beginning, is now, and will be forever. Amen.

Hymn

You, O Lord, I will obey;
  You with vast delight pursue;
Walking in your pleasant way,
  Glad your dear commands to do.

Psalm 119:1-3

Blessed are those whose ways are blameless,
  who walk according to the law of the LORD.
Blessed are those who keep his statutes
  and seek him with all their heart—
they do no wrong
  but follow his ways.

Prayer

Help us, O Lord, to express our love for you not only by learning your ways but also by walking in them.

Psalm 119:9-14

How can a young person stay on the path of purity?
  By living according to your word.
I seek you with all my heart;
  do not let me stray from your commands.
I have hidden your word in my heart
  that I might not sin against you.

Praise be to you, LORD;
>   teach me your decrees.
With my lips I recount
>   all the laws that come from your mouth.
I rejoice in following your statutes
>   as one rejoices in great riches.

Prayer

Assist us with your love, O Father, to keep your commandments. Grant each of us a heart that is willing and obedient like that of your Son, Jesus Christ, our Lord.

Scripture Reading (Optional)   1 John 2:3-6

Reflections from Augustine

There are two things that lead to sin: either we do not yet know our duty or we do not perform the duty we know. The former is the sin of ignorance; the latter of weakness. Now it is our duty to struggle against these things, but we will certainly be beaten in the fight unless we are helped by God, not only to see our duty but also, once we see it, to make the love of righteousness stronger in us than the love of earthly things. Indeed, the eager longing after earthly things, or the fear of losing them, leads us with our eyes open into known sin. (*Enchiridion*, chap. 81)

(Offer personal prayers.)

The Lord's Prayer

Dismissal

Guide us in the way of self-giving love, O Father, so that we may follow in the path of your Son, Christ Jesus, through whom we offer this our prayer. Amen.

DAY 4 † Evening Prayer

Self-Examination

(Reflect on the day, using the following questions as a guide, confess any departures from the law of love, and ask God for forgiveness.)

- Have I acknowledged my dependence on God by accepting his gift of a weekly day of rest—a sabbath day?
- Have I regularly gathered with other Christ-followers to praise and worship God?

Opening

O God, come to my assistance; O Lord, make haste to help me.
(Ps. 69:2, DRA)

Glory to the Father, and to the Son, and to the Holy Spirit: as it was in the beginning, is now, and will be forever. Amen.

Luke 1:54-55

[The Lord] has helped his servant Israel,
    remembering to be merciful
to Abraham and his descendants forever,
    just as he promised our ancestors.

Intercessions

(Offer personal prayers.)

Lord's Prayer

Dismissal

Enfold us in your arms, O Father, as we sleep, and calm our hearts so that we may rest safe and secure knowing you are near us, through Christ Jesus, our Lord. Amen.

Personal Meditations

DAY 5 † Morning Prayer

O Lord, open my lips, and my mouth will declare your praise. (Ps. 51:15, NRSV)

Psalm 100:4-5

Enter [the LORD's] gates with thanksgiving
and his courts with praise;
give thanks to him and praise his name.
For the LORD is good and his love endures forever;
his faithfulness continues through all generations.

Glory to the Father, and to the Son, and to the Holy Spirit: as it was in the beginning, is now, and will be forever. Amen.

Hymn

A mighty Fortress is our God,
A Bulwark never failing;
Our Helper he, amid the flood
Of mortal ills prevailing.

Psalm 18:1-3

I love you, LORD, my strength.
The LORD is my rock, my fortress and my deliverer;
my God is my rock, in whom I take refuge,
my shield and the horn of my salvation, my stronghold.
I called to the LORD, who is worthy of praise,
and I have been saved from my enemies.

Prayer

Almighty God, we praise you for your unshakeable love with which you surround us each day. No matter what assails us, you are always by our side.

Psalm 18:16-19

[The LORD] reached down from on high and took hold of me;
 he drew me out of deep waters.
He rescued me from my powerful enemy,
 from my foes, who were too strong for me.
They confronted me in the day of my disaster,
 but the LORD was my support.
He brought me out into a spacious place;
 he rescued me because he delighted in me.

Prayer

We lift our hearts in adoration to you, O God, for through the sacrifice of your Son, Jesus, we are no longer captives to sin and death. You have delivered our souls from these enemies.

Scripture Reading (Optional)   Romans 8:1-4

Reflections from Augustine

After the fall a more abundant exercise of God's mercy was required, because the will itself had to be freed from the bondage in which it was held by sin and death. And the will does not owe its freedom in any way to itself but solely to the grace of God that comes by faith in Jesus Christ. Thus the very will—through which we accept all the other gifts of God that lead us on to his eternal gift—is itself prepared by the Lord. (*Enchiridion*, chap. 106)

(Offer personal prayers.)

The Lord's Prayer

Dismissal

O Father, make us ambassadors of the freedom you have granted us through your Son. Help us to share this gift with others, through Christ Jesus, our Lord. Amen.

DAY 5 † Evening Prayer

Self-Examination

(Reflect on the day, using the following questions as a guide, confess any departures from the law of love, and ask God for forgiveness.)

- Have I treated my parents with dignity and respect?
- Have I encouraged and behaved kindly toward my children or others under my care?

Opening

O God, come to my assistance; O Lord, make haste to help me.
(Ps. 69:2, DRA)

Glory to the Father, and to the Son, and to the Holy Spirit: as it was in the beginning, is now, and will be forever. Amen.

Luke 2:29-32

Sovereign Lord, as you have promised,
   you may now dismiss your servant in peace.
For my eyes have seen your salvation,
   which you have prepared in the sight of all nations:
a light for revelation to the Gentiles,
   and the glory of your people Israel.

Intercessions

(Offer personal prayers.)

Lord's Prayer

Dismissal

Turn our hearts heavenward, O God, so that our thoughts before slumber may be of you, through Christ, our Savior and Lord. Amen.

Personal Meditations

DAY 6 † Morning Prayer

O Lord, open my lips, and my mouth will declare your praise. (Ps. 51:15, NRSV)

Psalm 67:1-2

May God be gracious to us and bless us
    and make his face shine on us—
so that your ways may be known on earth,
    your salvation among all nations.

Glory to the Father, and to the Son, and to the Holy Spirit: as it was in the beginning, is now, and will be forever. Amen.

Hymn

Fill up my life, O Lord, my God,
    In every part with praise,
That my whole being may proclaim
    Your being and your ways.

Psalm 16:5-8

LORD, you alone are my portion and my cup;
    you make my lot secure.
The boundary lines have fallen for me in pleasant places;
    surely I have a delightful inheritance.
I will praise the LORD, who counsels me;
    even at night my heart instructs me.
I keep my eyes always on the LORD.
    With him at my right hand, I will not be shaken.

Prayer

Keep us centered on you, O Lord, our true Inheritance. Even in our darkest moments you are there to guide and support us with your steadfast love.

Psalm 22:27-28

All the ends of the earth
    will remember and turn to the LORD,
and all the families of the nations
    will bow down before him,
for dominion belongs to the LORD
    and he rules over the nations.

Prayer

O holy Christ, we adore you for your sacrifice on behalf of the world. Through your upraised cross you are drawing people from all nations to yourself.

Scripture Reading (Optional)   Galatians 3:6-14

Reflections from Augustine

The church herself speaks out of the mouth of a mother's love: "You view me with wonder because I am bearing fruit and increasing throughout the whole world; however, there was a time when I was not as you now see me. But God said to Abraham, 'In your seed shall all nations be blessed.' When God blessed Abraham, he gave the promise of me, for in the blessing of Christ I have been poured out throughout all nations. And Christ is indeed the Seed of Abraham, as the order of successive generations clearly shows." ("Concerning Faith of Things Not Seen," sec. 5)

(Offer personal prayers.)

The Lord's Prayer

Dismissal

O God, make us channels of your grace today so that others will see the love of Christ in us and be drawn to love and worship you. This we ask in the name of that same Jesus, your beloved Son. Amen.

DAY 6 † Evening Prayer

Self-Examination

(Reflect on the day, using the following questions as a guide, confess any departures from the law of love, and ask God for forgiveness.)

- Have I exercised care in my daily activities to ensure that the lives of others are not put at risk?
- Have I thought, spoken, or written anything spiteful or mean about my neighbor?

Opening

O God, come to my assistance; O Lord, make haste to help me.
(Ps. 69:2, DRA)

Glory to the Father, and to the Son, and to the Holy Spirit: as it was in the beginning, is now, and will be forever. Amen.

Isaiah 12:2

Surely God is my salvation;
    I will trust and not be afraid.
The LORD, the LORD himself, is my strength and my defense;
    he has become my salvation.

Intercessions

(Offer personal prayers.)

Lord's Prayer

Dismissal

Protect us in our sleep, O God, and awaken us at the break of day ready to lift our hearts in joyful praise to you, through Christ Jesus, our Lord. Amen.

Personal Meditations

DAY 7 † Morning Prayer

O Lord, open my lips, and my mouth will declare your praise. (Ps. 51:15, NRSV)

Psalm 67:3-4

May the peoples praise you, God;
may all the peoples praise you.
May the nations be glad and sing for joy,
for you rule the peoples with equity
and guide the nations of the earth.

Glory to the Father, and to the Son, and to the Holy Spirit: as it was in the beginning, is now, and will be forever. Amen.

Hymn

Praise, my soul, the King of heaven;
To his feet your tribute bring.
Ransomed, healed, restored, forgiven,
Evermore his praises sing.

Psalm 116:1-4

I love the LORD, for he heard my voice;
he heard my cry for mercy.
Because he turned his ear to me,
I will call on him as long as I live.
The cords of death entangled me,
the anguish of the grave came over me;
I was overcome by distress and sorrow.
Then I called on the name of the LORD:
"LORD, save me!"

Prayer

We love and worship you, Heavenly Father, for you have raised us from the pit of death to new life, even as Christ, your Son, was raised. You heard our cry for help and rescued us from sin's deadly grip.

Psalm 116:5-7

The LORD is gracious and righteous;
  our God is full of compassion.
The LORD protects the unwary;
  when I was brought low, he saved me.
Return to your rest, my soul,
  for the LORD has been good to you.

Prayer

O God, our gracious Savior, help us to rely on you more and more so that with grateful and loving hearts we may better serve you and share your goodness with others.

Scripture Reading (Optional)   2 Corinthians 5:17

Reflections from Augustine

We shall be made truly free, then, when God fashions us, that is, forms and creates us anew, not as people—for he has done that already—but as good people, which his grace is now doing, that we may be a new creation in Christ Jesus. This is in accord with what the psalmist says: "Create in me a clean heart, O God." We know that God had already created his heart, as far as the physical structure of the human heart is concerned, but the psalmist prays for the renewal of the life that was still lingering in his heart. (*Enchiridion*, chap. 31)

(Offer personal prayers.)

The Lord's Prayer

Dismissal

Accompany us today, O God, in all our activities. Keep our hearts pure and centered on you so that we may bring glory and honor to your name, through Christ Jesus, our Lord. Amen.

DAY 7 † Evening Prayer

Self-Examination
(Reflect on the day, using the following questions as a guide, confess any departures from the law of love, and ask God for forgiveness.)
- Have I been unfaithful to God by allowing people, possessions, or activities to supersede my relationship with him?
- Have I been unfaithful to my spouse or disloyal to those closest to me in my thoughts, words, or deeds?

Opening
O God, come to my assistance; O Lord, make haste to help me.
(Ps. 69:2, DRA)

Glory to the Father, and to the Son, and to the Holy Spirit: as it was in the beginning, is now, and will be forever. Amen.

Isaiah 12:4
Give praise to the LORD, proclaim his name;
    make known among the nations what he has done,
    and proclaim that his name is exalted.

Intercessions
(Offer personal prayers.)

Lord's Prayer

Dismissal
As night deepens, O God, we take our rest, confident of your watchful care and steadfast love, through Christ Jesus, our Lord. Amen.

Personal Meditations

DAY 8 † Morning Prayer

O Lord, open my lips, and my mouth will declare your praise. (Ps. 51:15, NRSV)

Psalm 67:5-7

May the peoples praise you, God;
> may all the peoples praise you.
The land yields its harvest;
> God, our God, blesses us.
May God bless us still,
> so that all the ends of the earth will fear him.

Glory to the Father, and to the Son, and to the Holy Spirit: as it was in the beginning, is now, and will be forever. Amen.

Hymn

Let the whole creation cry:
Glory to the Lord on high!
Heaven and earth, awake and sing:
God is God and therefore King!

Psalm 148:1-6

Praise the LORD from the heavens;
> praise him in the heights above.
Praise him, all his angels;
> praise him, all his heavenly hosts.
Praise him, sun and moon;
> praise him, all you shining stars.
Praise him, you highest heavens
> and you waters above the skies.
Let them praise the name of the LORD,
> for at his command they were created,
and he established them for ever and ever—
> he issued a decree that will never pass away.

Prayer

Joining all creation, we praise you, O God, for you have created all things and through the sacrifice of your Son, Jesus, are bringing about their renewal.

Psalm 149:1-5

Sing to the LORD a new song,
>his praise in the assembly of his faithful people.
Let Israel rejoice in their Maker;
>let the people of Zion be glad in their King.
Let them praise his name with dancing
>and make music to him with timbrel and harp.
For the LORD takes delight in his people;
>he crowns the humble with victory.
Let his faithful people rejoice in this honor
>and sing for joy on their beds.

Prayer

We adore you, O God, for through Christ's blood you have given us victory over sin and death and made us into a new people to love and serve you.

Scripture Reading (Optional)   Acts 17:24-31

Reflections from Augustine

It is enough for the Christian to believe that the only cause of all created things, whether heavenly or earthly, whether visible or invisible, is the goodness of the Creator, the one true God; that nothing exists (except for himself) that does not derive its existence from him; and that he is the Trinity—namely, the Father, the Son begotten of the Father, and the Holy Spirit proceeding from the same Father, but one and the same Spirit of Father and Son. (*Enchiridion*, chap. 9)

(Offer personal prayers.)

The Lord's Prayer

Dismissal

O wonderful Creator, may we be vessels of praise to you for the beauty and goodness of all you have made and for the redemption and re-creation of our souls, through Christ Jesus, our Lord. Amen.

DAY 8 † Evening Prayer

Self-Examination

(Reflect on the day, using the following questions as a guide, confess any departures from the law of love, and ask God for forgiveness.)

- Have I behaved dishonestly at my work or occupation by misusing time or misappropriating resources?
- Have I selfishly maneuvered other people to achieve personal goals?

Opening

O God, come to my assistance; O Lord, make haste to help me.
(Ps. 69:2, DRA)

Glory to the Father, and to the Son, and to the Holy Spirit: as it was in the beginning, is now, and will be forever. Amen.

Isaiah 12:5-6

Sing to the LORD, for he has done glorious things;
>	let this be known to all the world.
Shout aloud and sing for joy, people of Zion,
>	for great is the Holy One of Israel among you.

Intercessions

(Offer personal prayers.)

Lord's Prayer

Dismissal

O God, free us from all worries and concerns so that we may sleep untroubled and rise refreshed at the break of day, through Christ Jesus, our Lord. Amen.

Personal Meditations

DAY 9 † Morning Prayer

O Lord, open my lips, and my mouth will declare your praise. (Ps. 51:15, NRSV)

Psalm 24:1-2

The earth is the LORD's, and everything in it,
　　the world, and all who live in it;
for he founded it on the seas
　　and established it on the waters.

Glory to the Father, and to the Son, and to the Holy Spirit: as it was in the beginning, is now, and will be forever. Amen.

Hymn

Come, Holy Spirit, heavenly Dove,
　　With all your quickening powers;
Come, shed abroad a Savior's love,
　　And that shall kindle ours.

Psalm 25:4-7

Show me your ways, LORD,
　　teach me your paths.
Guide me in your truth and teach me,
　　for you are God my Savior,
　　and my hope is in you all day long.
Remember, LORD, your great mercy and love,
　　for they are from of old.
Do not remember the sins of my youth
　　and my rebellious ways;
according to your love remember me,
　　for you, LORD, are good.

Prayer

Heavenly Father, through your Holy Spirit, guide us in the narrow way that leads to paradise—the way of Christ Jesus, our Lord.

Psalm 9:7-10

The LORD reigns forever;
　　he has established his throne for judgment.
He rules the world in righteousness
　　and judges the peoples with equity.
The LORD is a refuge for the oppressed,
　　a stronghold in times of trouble.
Those who know your name trust in you,
　　for you, LORD, have never forsaken those who seek you.

Prayer

O Eternal God and King, you are the true and just Judge, the Defender of the weak and downtrodden. Help us when our cares weigh us down always to trust in you.

Scripture Reading (Optional)　　John 16:12-15

Reflections from Augustine

Seek to grow in the love that is poured out in your hearts by the Holy Spirit, who is given to you, so that fervent in spirit, and with a love for spiritual things, you can become acquainted with that spiritual light and that spiritual word that unspiritual people cannot appreciate. For no one can love what he or she does not know. But when someone loves what he or she does know, in however small a measure, by that same love that person is led on to a better and fuller knowledge. (*On the Gospel of St. John*, tractate 96, sec. 4)

(Offer personal prayers.)

The Lord's Prayer

Dismissal

Lead us with your Holy Spirit today, O Lord. Strengthen our faith, protect us from temptation, and deepen our knowledge of you, through Christ Jesus, our Lord. Amen.

DAY 9 † Evening Prayer

Self-Examination
(Reflect on the day, using the following questions as a guide, confess any departures from the law of love, and ask God for forgiveness.)
- Have I spoken about others truthfully and only out of a heart of love and compassion for their well-being?
- Have I avoided entertaining and spreading gossip and rumors?

Opening
O God, come to my assistance; O Lord, make haste to help me.
(Ps. 69:2, DRA)

Glory to the Father, and to the Son, and to the Holy Spirit: as it was in the beginning, is now, and will be forever. Amen.

Isaiah 55:6-7
Seek the LORD while he may be found;
　　call on him while he is near.
Let the wicked forsake their ways
　　and the unrighteous their thoughts.

Intercessions
(Offer personal prayers.)

Lord's Prayer

Dismissal
Attend to us, O loving Father, as we sleep so that we may know you are near and that we are not alone, through your Son, Christ Jesus, our wonderful Lord. Amen.

Personal Meditations

DAY 10 † Morning Prayer

Psalm 24:3-5

Who may ascend the mountain of the LORD?
   Who may stand in his holy place?
The one who has clean hands and a pure heart,
   who does not trust in an idol
   or swear by a false god.
They will receive blessing from the LORD
   and vindication from God their Savior.

Glory to the Father, and to the Son, and to the Holy Spirit: as it was in the beginning, is now, and will be forever. Amen.

Hymn

To God be the glory, great things he has done;
So loved he the world that he gave us his Son,
Who yielded his life an atonement for sin,
And opened the lifegate that all may go in.

Psalm 28:6-7

Praise be to the LORD,
   for he has heard my cry for mercy.
The LORD is my strength and my shield;
   my heart trusts in him, and he helps me.
My heart leaps for joy,
   and with my song I praise him.

Prayer

We recall, O God, your help in times gone by and rejoice in thankful praise for your unwavering strength and faithfulness.

Psalm 36:7-9

How priceless is your unfailing love, O God!
People take refuge in the shadow of your wings.
They feast on the abundance of your house;
you give them drink from your river of delights.
For with you is the fountain of life;
in your light we see light.

Prayer

O God, who is Love, we bless your name, for through Christ, the Fountain of living water, you send the streams of eternal life.

Scripture Reading (Optional)   John 7:37-39

Reflections from Augustine

Christ has promised us eternal life, where we shall have no fear, where we shall not be troubled, from whence we shall never depart, and where we shall not die. It is where there is neither grieving for those who have died before us nor a hoping for those who will come after us. This is what Christ promised to us who love him and glow with the charity of the Holy Spirit. (*On the Gospel of St. John*, tractate 32, sec. 9)

(Offer personal prayers.)

The Lord's Prayer

Dismissal

Help us to be trustworthy bearers of the message of eternal life, the gospel of your Son, to our families, coworkers, and friends, through Christ Jesus, our Lord. Amen.

DAY 10 † Evening Prayer

Self-Examination

(Reflect on the day, using the following questions as a guide, confess any departures from the law of love, and ask God for forgiveness.)
- Have I been envious of the success or possessions of others?
- Have I striven to accumulate more property to attain a higher standing among my neighbors?

Opening

O God, come to my assistance; O Lord, make haste to help me.
(Ps. 69:2, DRA)

Glory to the Father, and to the Son, and to the Holy Spirit: as it was in the beginning, is now, and will be forever. Amen.

Isaiah 55:7-8

Let [the wicked] turn to the LORD, and he will have mercy on them,
    and to our God, for he will freely pardon.
"For my thoughts are not your thoughts,
    neither are your ways my ways,"
    declares the LORD.

Intercessions

(Offer personal prayers.)

Lord's Prayer

Dismissal

Remind us, O God, as this day ends, of the hope of life everlasting for those whose sins are forgiven through the sacrifice of your Son, Christ Jesus, our Lord. Amen.

Personal Meditations

DAY 11 † Morning Prayer

O Lord, open my lips, and my mouth will declare your praise. (Ps. 51:15, NRSV)

Psalm 95:1-2

Come, let us sing for joy to the LORD;
    let us shout aloud to the Rock of our salvation.
Let us come before him with thanksgiving
    and extol him with music and song.

Glory to the Father, and to the Son, and to the Holy Spirit: as it was in the beginning, is now, and will be forever. Amen.

Hymn

Your nature, gracious Lord, impart;
    Come quickly from above;
Write your new name upon my heart,
    Your new, best name of Love.

Psalm 119:29-30

Keep me from deceitful ways;
    be gracious to me and teach me your law.
I have chosen the way of faithfulness;
    I have set my heart on your laws.

Prayer

O Lord, do not let us stray onto false paths. Only on the true Path, which is Christ, do we find life.

Psalm 119:35-37

Direct me in the path of your commands,
    for there I find delight.
Turn my heart toward your statutes
    and not toward selfish gain.
Turn my eyes away from worthless things;
    preserve my life according to your word.

Prayer

Keep our hearts and minds turned to you and your ways, O Lord. Help us through your Holy Spirit not to let anything distract us from the way of self-giving love.

Scripture Reading (Optional)   1 Timothy 1:3-7

Reflections from Augustine

The end of every commandment is charity; that is, every commandment has love for its aim. But whatever is done either through fear of punishment or from some other carnal motive, and has not for its principle that love that the Spirit of God sheds abroad in the heart, is not done as it ought to be done, however it may appear to others. For this love embraces both the love of God and the love of our neighbor, and "on these two commandments hang all the law and the prophets" and, we may add, the gospel and the apostles. For it is from these that we hear this voice: The end of the commandment is charity, and God is love. (*Enchiridion*, chap. 121)

(Offer personal prayers.)

The Lord's Prayer

Dismissal

Open our eyes, Heavenly Father, to the brokenness of others so that we may share your love with them, through Christ Jesus, our Lord. Amen.

DAY 11 † Evening Prayer

Self-Examination

(Reflect on the day, using the following questions as a guide, confess any departures from the law of love, and ask God for forgiveness.)

- Have I behaved humbly before other people, giving God glory for my talents and gifts?
- Have I used my gifts and resources to further the work of the kingdom?

Opening

O God, come to my assistance; O Lord, make haste to help me.
(Ps. 69:2, DRA)

Glory to the Father, and to the Son, and to the Holy Spirit: as it was in the beginning, is now, and will be forever. Amen.

Isaiah 60:1-2

Arise, shine, for your light has come,
    and the glory of the LORD rises upon you.
See, darkness covers the earth
    and thick darkness is over the peoples,
but the LORD rises upon you
    and his glory appears over you.

Intercessions

(Offer personal prayers.)

Lord's Prayer

Dismissal

As the darkness of night surrounds us, O Holy One, illuminate our hearts with the assurance of your loving presence. Through Christ Jesus we pray. Amen.

Personal Meditations

DAY 12 † Morning Prayer

O Lord, open my lips, and my mouth will declare your praise. (Ps. 51:15, NRSV)

Psalm 95:6-7

Come, let us bow down in worship,
let us kneel before the LORD our Maker;
for he is our God
and we are the people of his pasture,
the flock under his care.

Glory to the Father, and to the Son, and to the Holy Spirit: as it was in the beginning, is now, and will be forever. Amen.

Hymn

I am thine, O Lord; I have heard thy voice,
And it told thy love to me.
But I long to rise in the arms of faith
And be closer drawn to thee.

Psalm 37:1-4

Do not fret because of those who are evil
or be envious of those who do wrong;
for like the grass they will soon wither,
like green plants they will soon die away.
Trust in the LORD and do good;
dwell in the land and enjoy safe pasture.
Take delight in the LORD,
and he will give you the desires of your heart.

Prayer

Keep us mindful, O God, that though evildoers may prosper, if we stay centered on you, through Christ, we will dwell with you forever.

Psalm 37:39-40

The salvation of the righteous comes from the LORD;
    he is their stronghold in time of trouble.
The LORD helps them and delivers them;
    he delivers them from the wicked and saves them,
    because they take refuge in him.

Prayer

Even if our enemies surround us, O God, we rejoice, for you are our Deliverer. Help us to love our persecutors even as Christ loved those who persecuted him.

Scripture Reading (Optional)   Luke 6:35-36

Reflections from Augustine

The patience of God still invites the wicked to repentance, even as the discipline of God educates the good to patience. And so, too, does the mercy of God embrace the good that it may cherish them, even as the severity of God arrests the wicked to punish them. To the divine providence it has seemed good to prepare in the world to come for the righteous good things, which the unrighteous shall not enjoy, and for the wicked evil things, by which the good shall not be tormented. But as for the good things of this life and its troubles, God has willed that these should be common to both. This he has done so that we might not excessively desire the things wicked people equally enjoy or shrink in fear from the troubles even good people often suffer. (*City of God*, bk. 1, chap. 8)

(Offer personal prayers.)

The Lord's Prayer

Dismissal

Empower us, O Lord, with your Holy Spirit to be kind and compassionate to all people, including those who oppose us. In your name we pray. Amen.

DAY 12 † Evening Prayer

Self-Examination

(Reflect on the day, using the following questions as a guide, confess any departures from the law of love, and ask God for forgiveness.)

- Have I been generous to those in need, giving graciously from my abundance?
- Have I been sincere in my desire to serve Christ and my neighbor by seeking opportunities to do so?

Opening

O God, come to my assistance; O Lord, make haste to help me.
(Ps. 69:2, DRA)

Glory to the Father, and to the Son, and to the Holy Spirit: as it was in the beginning, is now, and will be forever. Amen.

Exodus 15:2

The LORD is my strength and my defense;
> he has become my salvation.
He is my God, and I will praise him,
> my father's God, and I will exalt him.

Intercessions

(Offer personal prayers.)

Lord's Prayer

Dismissal

Fill our hearts, O God, as night deepens, with peaceful images of your kingdom, through Christ Jesus, our Lord. Amen.

Personal Meditations

DAY 13 † Morning Prayer

O Lord, open my lips, and my mouth will declare your praise. (Ps. 51:15, NRSV)

Psalm 100:1-2

Shout for joy to the LORD, all the earth.
>Worship the LORD with gladness;
>come before him with joyful songs.

Glory to the Father, and to the Son, and to the Holy Spirit: as it was in the beginning, is now, and will be forever. Amen.

Hymn

O for a thousand tongues to sing
>*My great Redeemer's praise,*
The glories of my God and King,
>*The triumphs of his grace!*

Psalm 31:19-20

How abundant are the good things
>that you have stored up for those who fear you,
that you bestow in the sight of all,
>on those who take refuge in you.
In the shelter of your presence you hide them
>from all human intrigues;
you keep them safe in your dwelling
>from accusing tongues.

Prayer

As we serve you, O God, we praise you for your Holy Spirit, who consoles, empowers, and guides us, even when people attack us and speak evil against us.

Psalm 92:1-3

It is good to praise the LORD
　　and make music to your name, O Most High,
proclaiming your love in the morning
　　and your faithfulness at night,
to the music of the ten-stringed lyre
　　and the melody of the harp.

Prayer

We lavishly praise you, O gracious God, for through the gift of your Son you have freed us from sin and death and are renewing all creation. Your love and faithfulness are without end.

Scripture Reading (Optional)　Philippians 4:4-7

Reflections from Augustine

Let my soul praise you, that it may love you; and let it confess your own mercies to you, that it may praise you. Your whole creation does not cease, nor is it silent, in your praises. The human spirit by its own voice directs praise to you, and animals and physical things direct praise to you by the voices of those meditating on them. This is all so that our souls may from their weariness arise toward you, leaning on those things you have made and passing on to you, who has wonderfully made them, and there is there for us refreshment and true strength. (*Confessions*, 5.1.1)

(Offer personal prayers.)

The Lord's Prayer

Dismissal

We love and adore you, almighty God, for your protection and your many blessings. Today make us blessings to our family, friends, and neighbors— to all we meet, through Christ Jesus, your Son. Amen.

DAY 13 † Evening Prayer

Self-Examination

(Reflect on the day, using the following questions as a guide, confess any departures from the law of love, and ask God for forgiveness.)

- Have I welcomed strangers into my company with wholehearted interest and kindness?
- Have I taken time to listen and show compassion to the grieving and suffering?

Opening

O God, come to my assistance; O Lord, make haste to help me.
(Ps. 69:2, DRA)

Glory to the Father, and to the Son, and to the Holy Spirit: as it was in the beginning, is now, and will be forever. Amen.

Exodus 15:13

In your unfailing love you will lead
    the people you have redeemed.
In your strength you will guide them
    to your holy dwelling.

Intercessions

(Offer personal prayers.)

Lord's Prayer

Dismissal

With wholehearted gratitude, Father, for all the good things you bestowed on us this day, we take our slumber, confident of your watchful presence throughout the night. This we pray in the name of your Son, Christ Jesus. Amen.

Personal Meditations

DAY 14 † Morning Prayer

O Lord, open my lips, and my mouth will declare your praise. (Ps. 51:15, NRSV)

Psalm 100:3

Know that the LORD is God.
>It is he who made us, and we are his;
>we are his people, the sheep of his pasture.

Glory to the Father, and to the Son, and to the Holy Spirit: as it was in the beginning, is now, and will be forever. Amen.

Hymn

Come to the Light; 'tis shining for thee.
Sweetly the Light has dawned upon me.
Once I was blind, but now I can see.
The Light of the world is Jesus.

Psalm 30:4-5

Sing the praises of the LORD, you his faithful people;
>praise his holy name.
For his anger lasts only a moment,
>but his favor lasts a lifetime;
weeping may stay for the night,
>but rejoicing comes in the morning.

Prayer

We adore you, O Christ Jesus, for your entrance into our lives is like the brightness of dawn piercing the darkness of night. You have illumined us with your life-giving love.

Psalm 32:1-3, 5

Blessed is the one
>whose transgressions are forgiven,
>whose sins are covered.

Blessed is the one
> whose sin the LORD does not count against them
> and in whose spirit is no deceit.

When I kept silent,
> my bones wasted away
> through my groaning all day long.

. . . .

Then I acknowledged my sin to you
> and did not cover up my iniquity.

I said, "I will confess
> my transgressions to the LORD."

And you forgave
> the guilt of my sin.

Prayer

Great are you, O Lord God, for you are merciful and do not delay in forgiving those who sincerely confess their sins and turn their hearts to you.

Scripture Reading (Optional)   2 Corinthians 7:9-10

Reflections from Augustine

The mercy of God is never to be despaired of by those who truly repent, each according to the measure of his or her sin. And in the act of repentance, where a crime has been committed serious enough to cut off the sinner from the body of Christ, we are not to take account so much of the measure of time [the church requires that person to be a penitent] as of the measure of that person's sorrow, for a broken and a contrite heart God does not despise. (*Enchiridion*, chap. 65)

(Offer personal prayers.)

The Lord's Prayer

Dismissal

As people, O merciful God, whom you have graciously forgiven, help us daily to be graciously forgiving, through Christ, our Lord. Amen.

DAY 14 † Evening Prayer

Self-Examination

(Reflect on the day, using the following questions as a guide, confess any departures from the law of love, and ask God for forgiveness.)
- Have I displayed genuine joy for the blessings others receive?
- Have I attempted to be a blessing to those who dislike and oppose me?

Opening

O God, come to my assistance; O Lord, make haste to help me.
(Ps. 69:2, DRA)

Glory to the Father, and to the Son, and to the Holy Spirit: as it was in the beginning, is now, and will be forever. Amen.

Exodus 15:17-18

You will bring [your people] in and plant them
    on the mountain of your inheritance—
the place, LORD, you made for your dwelling,
    the sanctuary, Lord, your hands established.
The LORD reigns
    for ever and ever.

Intercessions

(Offer personal prayers.)

Lord's Prayer

Dismissal

Lull us to sleep, O Composer of our souls, with the sweet song of your loving presence and raise us at dawn ready to serve you and others, through Christ Jesus, our Lord. Amen.

Personal Meditations

DAY 15 † Morning Prayer

O Lord, open my lips, and my mouth will declare your praise. (Ps. 51:15, NRSV)

Psalm 100:4-5

Enter [the LORD's] gates with thanksgiving
    and his courts with praise;
        give thanks to him and praise his name.
For the LORD is good and his love endures forever;
    his faithfulness continues through all generations.

Glory to the Father, and to the Son, and to the Holy Spirit: as it was in the beginning, is now, and will be forever. Amen.

Hymn

Praise God, who reigns on high,
    The Lord whom we adore,
The Father, Son, and Holy Ghost,
    One God forevermore.

Psalm 63:1-3

You, God, are my God,
    earnestly I seek you;
I thirst for you,
    my whole being longs for you,
in a dry and parched land
    where there is no water.

I have seen you in the sanctuary
    and beheld your power and your glory.
Because your love is better than life,
    my lips will glorify you.

Prayer

We lift our hearts in loving praise to you, O God, for when we are drained, having no personal reserves, you come to us like cool water to parched lips and refresh our souls.

Psalm 150:1-3, 6

Praise the LORD.
Praise God in his sanctuary;
    praise him in his mighty heavens.
Praise him for his acts of power;
    praise him for his surpassing greatness.
Praise him with the sounding of the trumpet,
    praise him with the harp and lyre.

. . . .

Let everything that has breath praise the LORD.

Prayer

Almighty God, we call all creation to love and adore you, for you have made all things and have provided for their redemption through the blood of your Son, Christ Jesus, our Lord.

Scripture Reading (Optional)   Jeremiah 32:17-20

Reflections from Augustine

Let your works praise you, that we may love you; and let us love you, that your works may praise you. Indeed your works exist in time, with a beginning and an end—rising and setting, growing and decaying, having form and lacking perfection. They have thus their successions of morning and evening, partly hidden, partly apparent; for they were made from nothing by you, not of you, nor of any matter not belonging to you, or from anything created before. (*Confessions,* 13.33.48)

(Offer personal prayers.)

The Lord's Prayer

Dismissal

Help us this day, O Creator, to see afresh the beauty of all you have made so that our hearts may be lifted in joy and adoration to you, through your beloved Son, Christ Jesus, our Lord. Amen.

DAY 15 † Evening Prayer

Self-Examination

(Reflect on the day, using the following questions as a guide, confess any departures from the law of love, and ask God for forgiveness.)

- Have I treated everyone with dignity regardless of social or economic status?
- Have I sought to build warmhearted relationships with people having different backgrounds from myself?

Opening

O God, come to my assistance; O Lord, make haste to help me.
(Ps. 69:2, DRA)

Glory to the Father, and to the Son, and to the Holy Spirit: as it was in the beginning, is now, and will be forever. Amen.

Revelation 4:8

"Holy, holy, holy
is the Lord God Almighty,"
who was, and is, and is to come.

Intercessions

(Offer personal prayers.)

Lord's Prayer

Dismissal

We bless you, O God, as the day ends for shepherding us through its many challenges. You are the ever-faithful Caretaker of our souls, through Christ, our Lord. Amen.

Personal Meditations

DAY 16 † Morning Prayer

O Lord, open my lips, and my mouth will declare your praise. (Ps. 51:15, NRSV)

Psalm 67:1-2

May God be gracious to us and bless us
    and make his face shine on us—
so that your ways may be known on earth,
    your salvation among all nations.

Glory to the Father, and to the Son, and to the Holy Spirit: as it was in the beginning, is now, and will be forever. Amen.

Hymn

O to be like thee, full of compassion,
    Loving, forgiving, tender and kind,
Helping the helpless, cheering the fainting,
    Seeking the wandering sinner to find.

Psalm 41:1-3

Blessed are those who have regard for the weak;
    the LORD delivers them in times of trouble.
The LORD protects and preserves them—
    they are counted among the blessed in the land—
    he does not give them over to the desire of their foes.
The LORD sustains them on their sickbed
    and restores them from their bed of illness.

Prayer

O Lord Jesus, open our eyes so we can see you in the faces of the needy. Stir our hearts to seek and do what is best for them.

Psalm 52:8-9

I am like an olive tree
  flourishing in the house of God;
I trust in God's unfailing love
  for ever and ever.
For what you have done I will always praise you
  in the presence of your faithful people.
And I will hope in your name,
  for your name is good.

Prayer

Help us, O loving Father, to rely on you and not on ourselves, for only you
can give us the enduring strength and vitality needed for evangelism and
compassionate service.

Scripture Reading (Optional)   Mark 12:28-34

Reflections from Augustine

The love of God comes first in the order of enjoying; but in the order
of doing, the love of our neighbor comes first. For he who gave you this
commandment of love in two precepts did not charge you to love your
neighbor first, and then God, but first God, afterward your neighbor. You,
however, since you do not yet see God, prepare yourself to see him by loving your neighbor; by loving your neighbor you purify your eye for seeing
God. (*On the Gospel of St. John*, tractate 17, sec. 8)

(Offer personal prayers.)

The Lord's Prayer

Dismissal

Cause our love for you, O God, to overflow from our hearts in generous
acts of kindness and mercy to our neighbors, through Christ Jesus, our
Lord. Amen.

DAY 16 † Evening Prayer

Self-Examination

(Reflect on the day, using the following questions as a guide, confess any departures from the law of love, and ask God for forgiveness.)

- Have I left my vindication to God when wronged by others?
- Have I reached out to my enemies to meet their needs and care for their well-being?

Opening

O God, come to my assistance; O Lord, make haste to help me.
(Ps. 69:2, DRA)

Glory to the Father, and to the Son, and to the Holy Spirit: as it was in the beginning, is now, and will be forever. Amen.

Revelation 4:11

You are worthy, our Lord and God,
　　to receive glory and honor and power,
for you created all things,
　　and by your will they were created
　　and have their being.

Intercessions

(Offer personal prayers.)

Lord's Prayer

Dismissal

We take our rest, almighty God, knowing you are the Creator and King of all things. You faithfully sustain us with your all-sufficient love, through Christ, your Son. Amen.

Personal Meditations

DAY 17 † Morning Prayer

O Lord, open my lips, and my mouth will declare your praise. (Ps. 51:15, NRSV)

Psalm 67:3-4

May the peoples praise you, God;
>   may all the peoples praise you.
May the nations be glad and sing for joy,
>   for you rule the peoples with equity
>   and guide the nations of the earth.

Glory to the Father, and to the Son, and to the Holy Spirit: as it was in the beginning, is now, and will be forever. Amen.

Hymn

We've a message to give to the nations,
>   *That the Lord who reigns above*
Has sent us his Son to save us
>   *And show us that God is love.*

Psalm 47:1-2, 6-7

Clap your hands, all you nations;
>   shout to God with cries of joy.
For the LORD Most High is awesome,
>   the great King over all the earth.

. . . .

Sing praises to God, sing praises;
>   sing praises to our King, sing praises.
For God is the King of all the earth;
>   sing to him a psalm of praise.

Prayer

Open our hearts, O mighty King, with a love for all people. Make us living invitations in word and deed to draw them into the realm of your love.

Psalm 48:9-11

Within your temple, O God,
    we meditate on your unfailing love.
Like your name, O God,
    your praise reaches to the ends of the earth;
    your right hand is filled with righteousness.
Mount Zion rejoices,
    the villages of Judah are glad
    because of your judgments.

Prayer

Christ Jesus, you have redeemed your temple, the church. Help it always to be a beacon of your love and righteousness to the entire world.

Scripture Reading (Optional)   1 Corinthians 3:16-17

Reflections from Augustine

God dwells in his temple—not the Holy Spirit only, but the Father also, and the Son. (The Son, speaking similarly, says of his own body, through which he was made Head of the church on earth ["that in all things he might have the preeminence"], "Destroy this temple, and in three days I will raise it up.") The temple of God, then, namely, of the Supreme Trinity as a whole, is the holy church, embracing in its full extent both heaven and earth. (*Enchiridion*, chap. 56)

(Offer personal prayers.)

The Lord's Prayer

Dismissal

O holy God, we are part of your temple, the church, and we ask that you strengthen us with your Holy Spirit so that we may conduct our lives so that all who see us may be moved to love and worship you, through Christ Jesus, our Lord. Amen.

DAY 17 † Evening Prayer

Self-Examination

(Reflect on the day, using the following questions as a guide, confess any departures from the law of love, and ask God for forgiveness.)

- Have I vigorously pursued doing good things for my brothers and sisters in Christ?
- Have I through word and deed encouraged other Christ-followers in their spiritual growth?

Opening

O God, come to my assistance; O Lord, make haste to help me.
(Ps. 69:2, DRA)

Glory to the Father, and to the Son, and to the Holy Spirit: as it was in the beginning, is now, and will be forever. Amen.

Revelation 5:9-10

[O Lamb,] with your blood you purchased for God
persons from every tribe and language and people and nation.
You have made them to be a kingdom and priests to serve our God,
and they will reign on the earth.

Intercessions

(Offer personal prayers.)

Lord's Prayer

Dismissal

O Lord of all, we retire at the close of day strengthened with the wonderful knowledge that we are not only subjects but also priests and rulers in your kingdom, through Christ. Amen.

Personal Meditations

DAY 18 † Morning Prayer

> O Lord, open my lips, and my mouth will declare your praise. (Ps. 51:15, NRSV)

Psalm 67:5-7

May the peoples praise you, God;
>   may all the peoples praise you.
The land yields its harvest;
>   God, our God, blesses us.
May God bless us still,
>   so that all the ends of the earth will fear him.

Glory to the Father, and to the Son, and to the Holy Spirit: as it was in the beginning, is now, and will be forever. Amen.

Hymn

O God, what offering shall I give
>   *To you, the Lord of earth and skies?*
My spirit, soul, and flesh receive,
>   *A holy, living sacrifice.*

Psalm 119:57-60

You are my portion, LORD;
>   I have promised to obey your words.
I have sought your face with all my heart;
>   be gracious to me according to your promise.
I have considered my ways
>   and have turned my steps to your statutes.
I will hasten and not delay
>   to obey your commands.

Prayer

Help us, O Lord, our God, to obey you heartily and quickly in all we do, for only you fulfill us. Your love surpasses anything we may have or desire.

Psalm 49:12-15

People, despite their wealth, do not endure;
    they are like the beasts that perish.
This is the fate of those who trust in themselves,
    and of their followers, who approve their sayings.

. . . .

Their forms will decay in the grave,
    far from their princely mansions.
But God will redeem me from the realm of the dead;
    he will surely take me to himself.

Prayer

Keep us from trusting in money or riches, O God, for that way ends in death. Only by trusting in you, through your Son, Christ Jesus, do we find life everlasting.

Scripture Reading (Optional)   Ephesians 2:1-10

Reflections from Augustine

A gift, unless it is wholly unearned, is not a gift at all. We are to understand, then, that our good deserts are themselves the gift of God, so that when these obtain the recompense of eternal life, it is simply grace given for grace. We, therefore, having been made upright, are unable to remain in our uprightness without divine help, though of our own mere will we could depart from it. (*Enchiridion*, chap. 107)

(Offer personal prayers.)

The Lord's Prayer

Dismissal

Magnify yourself in all the good we do, O Father, so that everyone will know that you are working through us, bestowing on those in need your gracious love and compassion, through Christ Jesus, your beloved Son. Amen.

DAY 18 † Evening Prayer

Self-Examination

(Reflect on the day, using the following questions as a guide, confess any departures from the law of love, and ask God for forgiveness.)

- Have I behaved patiently toward those who need my guidance and support?
- Have I been more careful to listen to God and my neighbor than to speak?

Opening

O God, come to my assistance; O Lord, make haste to help me.
(Ps. 69:2, DRA)

Glory to the Father, and to the Son, and to the Holy Spirit: as it was in the beginning, is now, and will be forever. Amen.

Revelation 5:12

Worthy is the Lamb, who was slain,
> to receive power and wealth and wisdom and strength
> and honor and glory and praise!

Intercessions

(Offer personal prayers.)

Lord's Prayer

Dismissal

We extol you, Heavenly Father, for through the sacrifice of your Son, the Lamb of God, you have saved us from our sins and granted us peace. We offer this, our prayer of praise, in the name of that same Son, Christ Jesus, our Lord. Amen.

Personal Meditations

DAY 19 † Morning Prayer

Psalm 24:1-2

The earth is the LORD's, and everything in it,
> the world, and all who live in it;
for he founded it on the seas
> and established it on the waters.

Glory to the Father, and to the Son, and to the Holy Spirit: as it was in the beginning, is now, and will be forever. Amen.

Hymn

Glory to the King of angels!
> *Glory to the church's King!*
Glory to the King of nations!
> *Heaven and earth, your praises bring!*

Psalm 66:1-4

Shout for joy to God, all the earth!
> Sing the glory of his name;
> make his praise glorious.
Say to God, "How awesome are your deeds!
> So great is your power
> that your enemies cringe before you.
All the earth bows down to you;
> they sing praise to you,
> they sing the praises of your name."

Prayer

We thank you, almighty Father, for your great salvation. Through Christ, your Son, you are renewing your people and bringing all creation under your loving rule.

Psalm 135:1-6

Praise the name of the LORD;
>praise him, you servants of the LORD,
you who minister in the house of the LORD,
>in the courts of the house of our God.
Praise the LORD, for the LORD is good;
>sing praise to his name, for that is pleasant.
For the LORD has chosen Jacob to be his own,
>Israel to be his treasured possession.
I know that the LORD is great,
>that our Lord is greater than all gods.
The LORD does whatever pleases him,
>in the heavens and on the earth,
>in the seas and all their depths.

Prayer

Gracious God, who is Lord over all, you have saved us and called us into your church. We praise you and bless your holy name for the great love you have bestowed on us.

Scripture Reading (Optional)   Deuteronomy 6:4-5

Reflections from Augustine

O God, you alone do I love, you alone I follow, you alone I seek, you alone am I prepared to serve, for you alone are Lord by a just title, and under your rule do I desire to be. Direct, I pray, and command whatever you will, but heal and open my ears, that I may hear your utterances. Heal and open my eyes, that I may see the signs of command. Drive delusion from me, that I may recognize you. Tell me where I must attend to behold you, and I hope that I shall do all things you may enjoin. (*Soliloquies*, 1.5)

(Offer personal prayers.)

The Lord's Prayer

Dismissal

We renew our devotion to you, O God; align our wills with yours so that people will clearly see your love in us, through Christ Jesus, our Lord. Amen.

DAY 19 † Evening Prayer

Self-Examination

(Reflect on the day, using the following questions as a guide, confess any departures from the law of love, and ask God for forgiveness.)

- Have I remembered to give thanks daily from a sincere heart for being included in the body of Christ?
- Have I approached my work and all my daily tasks from an attitude of gratitude and wholehearted obedience to Christ?

Opening

O God, come to my assistance; O Lord, make haste to help me.
(Ps. 69:2, DRA)

Glory to the Father, and to the Son, and to the Holy Spirit: as it was in the beginning, is now, and will be forever. Amen.

Revelation 5:13

To him who sits on the throne and to the Lamb
be praise and honor and glory and power,
for ever and ever!

Intercessions

(Offer personal prayers.)

Lord's Prayer

Dismissal

Keep us safe as we sleep, O Holy One, so that we may awaken and worship you again through our obedience and daily work, through your Son, Christ Jesus. Amen.

Personal Meditations

DAY 20 † Morning Prayer

O Lord, open my lips, and my mouth will declare your praise. (Ps. 51:15, NRSV)

Psalm 24:3-5

Who may ascend the mountain of the LORD?
>Who may stand in his holy place?

The one who has clean hands and a pure heart,
>who does not trust in an idol
>or swear by a false god.

They will receive blessing from the LORD
>and vindication from God their Savior.

Glory to the Father, and to the Son, and to the Holy Spirit: as it was in the beginning, is now, and will be forever. Amen.

Hymn

O give me, Lord, the tender heart
>*That trembles at the approach of sin.*
A godly fear of sin impart,
>*Implant, and root it deep within.*

Psalm 51:1-2

Have mercy on me, O God,
>according to your unfailing love;

according to your great compassion
>blot out my transgressions.

Wash away all my iniquity
>and cleanse me from my sin.

Prayer

Search our hearts, O Holy One, so that we may confess any sin. For the sake of your Son, Jesus, grant us true repentance and forgive us. Purify us, we pray, of every stain.

Psalm 40:4-5

Blessed is the one
>who trusts in the LORD,

who does not look to the proud,
>to those who turn aside to false gods.

Many, LORD my God,
>are the wonders you have done,
>the things you planned for us.

None can compare with you;
>were I to speak and tell of your deeds,
>they would be too many to declare.

Prayer

We praise you, Lord, for your marvelous acts of mercy and deliverance. Help us to respond to all you have done with obedient and loving hearts.

Scripture Reading (Optional)   Colossians 1:21-23

Reflections from Augustine

I will love you, O Lord, and thank you, and confess your name, because you have put away from me these so wicked and nefarious acts of mine. To your grace I attribute it, and to your mercy, that you have melted away my sin as it were ice. To your grace also I attribute that you have saved me from committing whatever evil I have not committed, for what might I not have committed, loving as I did the sin for the sin's sake? Indeed, all sins I have confessed have been pardoned me, both those that I committed by my own perverseness and those that, by your guidance, I committed not. (*Confessions*, 2.7.15)

(Offer personal prayers.)

The Lord's Prayer

Dismissal

With thankful hearts, O God, we begin the day, grateful for your forgiveness and for the new life you have granted us through your Son, Christ Jesus, our Lord. Amen.

DAY 20 † Evening Prayer

Self-Examination

(Reflect on the day, using the following questions as a guide, confess any departures from the law of love, and ask God for forgiveness.)

- Have I held true to Christ even at the cost of my reputation and livelihood?
- Have I allowed the Holy Spirit to rule in my life by avoiding activities leading to sin and embracing practices leading to Christlikeness?

Opening

O God, come to my assistance; O Lord, make haste to help me.
(Ps. 69:2, DRA)

Glory to the Father, and to the Son, and to the Holy Spirit: as it was in the beginning, is now, and will be forever. Amen.

Revelation 15:3

Great and marvelous are your deeds,
Lord God Almighty.
Just and true are your ways,
King of the nations.

Intercessions

(Offer personal prayers.)

Lord's Prayer

Dismissal

Night has come, and we entrust ourselves to your benevolent rule, O holy King. Through your Holy Spirit our fears are calmed, our hearts strengthened, and our bodies refreshed for another day, through Christ, our blessed Savior. Amen.

Personal Meditations

DAY 21 † Morning Prayer

O Lord, open my lips, and my mouth will declare your praise. (Ps. 51:15, NRSV)

Psalm 95:1-2

Come, let us sing for joy to the LORD;
    let us shout aloud to the Rock of our salvation.
Let us come before him with thanksgiving
    and extol him with music and song.

Glory to the Father, and to the Son, and to the Holy Spirit: as it was in the beginning, is now, and will be forever. Amen.

Hymn

O worship the King, all glorious above,
O gratefully sing his power and his love;
Our Shield and Defender, the Ancient of days,
Pavilioned in splendor and girded with praise.

Psalm 138:6-8

Though the LORD is exalted, he looks kindly on the lowly;
    though lofty, he sees them from afar.
Though I walk in the midst of trouble,
    you preserve my life.
You stretch out your hand against the anger of my foes;
    with your right hand you save me.
The LORD will vindicate me;
    your love, LORD, endures forever—
    do not abandon the works of your hands.

Prayer

Blessed are you, Lord God, for in your loving-kindness you reach down to us in our neediness. Help us to serve you with humble hearts filled with love and praise.

Psalm 139:1-3, 5-6

You have searched me, LORD,
and you know me.
You know when I sit and when I rise;
you perceive my thoughts from afar.
You discern my going out and my lying down;
you are familiar with all my ways.

. . . .

You hem me in behind and before,
and you lay your hand upon me.
Such knowledge is too wonderful for me,
too lofty for me to attain.

Prayer

How marvelous you are, almighty God, for you know everything about us
and care for us every moment of the day. We glorify you for surrounding
us with your love.

Scripture Reading (Optional)   1 Corinthians 13:8-12

Reflections from Augustine

Let me know you, O God, who knows me; let me know you, as I am
known. O Strength of my soul, enter into it and prepare it for yourself,
that you may have and hold it without "spot or wrinkle." This is my hope,
and "thus have I spoken"; and in this hope do I rejoice, when I rejoice
rightly. (*Confessions*, 10.1.1)

(Offer personal prayers.)

The Lord's Prayer

Dismissal

Increase our knowledge of you today, O God, so that we may become
authentic reflections of your compassion and love, through your beloved
Son, Christ Jesus, our Lord. Amen.

DAY 21 † Evening Prayer

Self-Examination

(Reflect on the day, using the following questions as a guide, confess any departures from the law of love, and ask God for forgiveness.)

- Have I regularly prayed for those who are ill or grieving?
- Have I sincerely attempted to help as well as intercede for the suffering?

Opening

O God, come to my assistance; O Lord, make haste to help me.
(Ps. 69:2, DRA)

Glory to the Father, and to the Son, and to the Holy Spirit: as it was in the beginning, is now, and will be forever. Amen.

Revelation 15:4

Who will not fear you, Lord,
  and bring glory to your name?
For you alone are holy.

Intercessions

(Offer personal prayers.)

Lord's Prayer

Dismissal

O holy God, we end this day in celebration of you, for we know you are our Protector and Healer. There is none that can compare to you. We praise your wonderful name, through your Son, Christ Jesus, our Lord. Amen.

Personal Meditations

DAY 22 † Morning Prayer

O Lord, open my lips, and my mouth will declare your praise. (Ps. 51:15, NRSV)

Psalm 95:6-7

Come, let us bow down in worship,
    let us kneel before the LORD our Maker;
for he is our God
    and we are the people of his pasture,
    the flock under his care.

Glory to the Father, and to the Son, and to the Holy Spirit: as it was in the beginning, is now, and will be forever. Amen.

Hymn

Holy God, we praise your name;
    Lord of all, we bow before you.
All on earth your scepter claim;
    All in heaven above adore you.

Psalm 29:1-4, 10-11

Ascribe to the LORD, you heavenly beings,
    ascribe to the LORD glory and strength.
Ascribe to the LORD the glory due his name;
    worship the LORD in the splendor of his holiness.
The voice of the LORD is over the waters;
    the God of glory thunders,
    the LORD thunders over the mighty waters.
The voice of the LORD is powerful;
    the voice of the LORD is majestic.

. . . .

The LORD sits enthroned over the flood;
    the LORD is enthroned as King forever.
The LORD gives strength to his people;
    the LORD blesses his people with peace.

Prayer

O Lord, we lift our hearts in adoration to you, for your power and rule are displayed in creation and in the strength and peace you give your people.

Psalm 8:1, 3-5

Lord, our Lord,
>how majestic is your name in all the earth!

. . . .

When I consider your heavens,
>the work of your fingers,

the moon and the stars,
>which you have set in place,

what is mankind that you are mindful of them,
>human beings that you care for them?

You have made them a little lower than the angels
>and crowned them with glory and honor.

Prayer

We magnify you, O Lord, for you created the vast cosmos, and though we are small and mortal, you have wonderfully made us and given us governance over your creation.

Scripture Reading (Optional)   Genesis 1:26-28

Reflections from Augustine

You, O Lord my God, who gave life to the infant, and a frame that you have endowed with senses, compacted with limbs, beautified with form, and, for its general good and safety, have introduced all vital energies—you command me to praise you for these things, "to give thanks to the Lord and to sing praise to your name, O Most High," for you are a God omnipotent and good. (*Confessions*, 1.7.12)

(Offer personal prayers.)

The Lord's Prayer

Dismissal

Holy Creator, empower us with your Holy Spirit to do the good for which you made us and for which you have now saved us, through Christ. Amen.

DAY 22 † Evening Prayer

Self-Examination
(Reflect on the day, using the following questions as a guide, confess any departures from the law of love, and ask God for forgiveness.)
- Have I spoken wisely and graciously to nonbelievers, always striving to build with them Christ-honoring relationships?
- Have I prayed fervently and worked diligently to assist other Christ-followers as they minister the gospel to others?

Opening
O God, come to my assistance; O Lord, make haste to help me.
(Ps. 69:2, DRA)

Glory to the Father, and to the Son, and to the Holy Spirit: as it was in the beginning, is now, and will be forever. Amen.

Revelation 15:4
All nations will come
    and worship before you, [O Lord,]
for your righteous acts have been revealed.

Intercessions
(Offer personal prayers.)

Lord's Prayer

Dismissal
As we begin our evening rest, Father, turn our thoughts to those who do not know you. Awaken us tomorrow with a fresh resolve to build sincere friendships that will introduce others to your love, through Christ, your Son. Amen.

Personal Meditations

DAY 23 † Morning Prayer

O Lord, open my lips, and my mouth will declare your praise. (Ps. 51:15, NRSV)

Psalm 100:1-2

Shout for joy to the LORD, all the earth.
Worship the LORD with gladness;
come before him with joyful songs.

Glory to the Father, and to the Son, and to the Holy Spirit: as it was in the beginning, is now, and will be forever. Amen.

Hymn

Praise the Lord! for he is glorious;
Never shall his promise fail.
God hath made his saints victorious;
Sin and death shall not prevail.

Psalm 57:8-11

Awake, my soul!
Awake, harp and lyre!
I will awaken the dawn.
I will praise you, Lord, among the nations;
I will sing of you among the peoples.
For great is your love, reaching to the heavens;
your faithfulness reaches to the skies.
Be exalted, O God, above the heavens;
let your glory be over all the earth.

Prayer

We celebrate you, O Father, with praises resounding throughout creation, for you have delivered us from sin and death and raised us to new life through Christ, your Son.

Psalm 65:1-4

> Praise awaits you, our God, in Zion;
>> to you our vows will be fulfilled.
> You who answer prayer,
>> to you all people will come.
> When we were overwhelmed by sins,
>> you forgave our transgressions.
> Blessed are those you choose
>> and bring near to live in your courts!
> We are filled with the good things of your house,
>> of your holy temple.

Prayer

We owe and offer you, O Lord, our love and praise for all the good things you have done but especially for forgiving our sins and granting us a close relationship with you.

Scripture Reading (Optional)   John 8:31-36

Reflections from Augustine

When we were servants of sin, we were free to sin and not free to do right. But when we were freed from sin, we became servants of righteousness. This is true freedom, for now we take pleasure in the righteous deed; this freedom is also a holy bondage, for we are obedient to the will of God. But where could we get this freedom to do right while we were in bondage and sold under sin if we were not redeemed by the One who has said, "If the Son shall make you free, you shall be free indeed"? (*Enchiridion*, chap. 30)

(Offer personal prayers.)

The Lord's Prayer

Dismissal

Now that you have freed us from the shackles of sin, O Holy One, send us out as your obedient ambassadors, serving others and telling them about your glorious kingdom, through Christ Jesus, our Lord. Amen.

DAY 23 † Evening Prayer

Self-Examination

(Reflect on the day, using the following questions as a guide, confess any departures from the law of love, and ask God for forgiveness.)
- Have I had impure thoughts because I have been unwise in what I have viewed and what I have read?
- Have I ignored the urgings of the Holy Spirit when confronted by temptation?

Opening

O God, come to my assistance; O Lord, make haste to help me.
(Ps. 69:2, DRA)

Glory to the Father, and to the Son, and to the Holy Spirit: as it was in the beginning, is now, and will be forever. Amen.

Revelation 19:1-2

Hallelujah!
Salvation and glory and power belong to our God,
for true and just are his judgments.

Intercessions

(Offer personal prayers.)

Lord's Prayer

Dismissal

O Gracious One, as our weariness draws us to our nightly slumber, fill our minds with thoughts of your great salvation that is at work in us, transforming us more and more into the image of your Son, through whom we offer this our prayer. Amen.

Personal Meditations

DAY 24 † Morning Prayer

O Lord, open my lips, and my mouth will declare your praise. (Ps. 51:15, NRSV)

Psalm 100:3

Know that the LORD is God.
>It is he who made us, and we are his;
>we are his people, the sheep of his pasture.

Glory to the Father, and to the Son, and to the Holy Spirit: as it was in the beginning, is now, and will be forever. Amen.

Hymn

Glory be to God on high,
>*And peace on earth descend;*
God comes down, he bows the sky,
>*And shows himself our Friend.*

Psalm 62:6-8

Truly [God] is my rock and my salvation;
>he is my fortress, I will not be shaken.
My salvation and my honor depend on God;
>he is my mighty rock, my refuge.
Trust in him at all times, you people;
>pour out your hearts to him,
>for God is our refuge.

Prayer

You alone, O God, are our sure Foundation. Help us to rely on you for our well-being and worth and not on our status or the regard of others.

Psalm 68:4-6

Sing to God, sing in praise of his name,
extol him who rides on the clouds;
rejoice before him—his name is the Lord.
A father to the fatherless, a defender of widows,
is God in his holy dwelling.
God sets the lonely in families,
he leads out the prisoners with singing;
but the rebellious live in a sun-scorched land.

Prayer

Blessed are you, O Lord God, for you surround orphans and widows with
your loving-kindness and lift the hearts of the sorrowful.

Scripture Reading (Optional)   Isaiah 46:3-4

Reflections from Augustine

O Lord our God, under the shadow of your wings let us hope; defend us,
and carry us. You will carry us both when little, and even to gray hairs will
you carry us; for our firmness, when it is you, then is it firmness; but when it
is our own, then it is infirmity. Our good lives always with you, from which
when we are averted we are perverted. Let us now, O Lord, return, that we
be not overturned, because with you our good lives without decline, which
good you yourself are. And we do not need to fear that we will not find a
place to return to because we fell away from it, for when we were absent,
our home—your eternity—fell not. (*Confessions*, 4.16.31)

(Offer personal prayers.)

The Lord's Prayer

Dismissal

Remake us, O God, so that we may become coworkers with you in loving
and caring for the weak and suffering. Transform us into channels of your
compassion and mercy, through Christ Jesus, our Savior and Lord. Amen.

DAY 24 † Evening Prayer

Self-Examination

(Reflect on the day, using the following questions as a guide, confess any departures from the law of love, and ask God for forgiveness.)

- Have I allowed the Holy Spirit control over my temperament so that my anger and personal dissatisfaction does not harm my relationships with others?
- Have I avoided using language that is not clean and edifying?

Opening

O God, come to my assistance; O Lord, make haste to help me. (Ps. 69:2, DRA)

Glory to the Father, and to the Son, and to the Holy Spirit: as it was in the beginning, is now, and will be forever. Amen.

Revelation 19:5

Praise our God,
>   all you his servants,
you who fear him,
>   both great and small!

Intercessions

(Offer personal prayers.)

Lord's Prayer

Dismissal

O Father, we close our eyes for our nightly rest with a deep love for you in our hearts and a gentle word of praise to you on our lips, through Christ Jesus, our Lord. Amen.

Personal Meditations

DAY 25 † Morning Prayer

O Lord, open my lips, and my mouth will declare your praise. (Ps. 51:15, NRSV)

Psalm 100:4-5

Enter [the LORD's] gates with thanksgiving
and his courts with praise;
give thanks to him and praise his name.
For the LORD is good and his love endures forever;
his faithfulness continues through all generations.

Glory to the Father, and to the Son, and to the Holy Spirit: as it was in the
beginning, is now, and will be forever. Amen.

Hymn

Sing praise to God who reigns above,
The God of all creation,
The God of power, the God of love,
The God of our salvation.

Psalm 119:89-93

Your word, LORD, is eternal;
it stands firm in the heavens.
Your faithfulness continues through all generations;
you established the earth, and it endures.
Your laws endure to this day,
for all things serve you.
If your law had not been my delight,
I would have perished in my affliction.
I will never forget your precepts,
for by them you have preserved my life.

Prayer

Praise to you, Christ Jesus, our Lord, for you are the Living Word,
through whom all things were created and our souls find true life and
enduring love.

Psalm 103:1-5

Praise the LORD, my soul;
    all my inmost being, praise his holy name.
Praise the LORD, my soul,
    and forget not all his benefits—
who forgives all your sins
    and heals all your diseases,
who redeems your life from the pit
    and crowns you with love and compassion,
who satisfies your desires with good things
    so that your youth is renewed like the eagle's.

Prayer

We give thanks to you, O God, for many are your blessings. Your love surrounds us with forgiveness, healing, and countless good things.

Scripture Reading (Optional)   Romans 3:21-26

Reflections from Augustine

The saints shall know more fully the benefits they have received by grace. Then, in contemplation of the actual facts, they shall see more clearly the meaning of the expression in the psalms, "I will sing of mercy and judgment," for it is only of unmerited mercy that any is redeemed and only in well-merited judgment that any is condemned. (*Enchiridion*, chap. 94)

(Offer personal prayers.)

The Lord's Prayer

Dismissal

Give us opportunity, O God, to tell others about your grace and mercy. May our words and actions proclaim your great salvation to the people we know and meet, through Christ Jesus, our Lord. Amen.

DAY 25 † Evening Prayer

Self-Examination
(Reflect on the day, using the following questions as a guide, confess any departures from the law of love, and ask God for forgiveness.)
- Have I been willing to sacrifice my own desires to maintain the unity and peace of my brothers and sisters in Christ?
- Have I been truthful in my dealings with all people, believers and nonbelievers alike?

Opening
O God, come to my assistance; O Lord, make haste to help me.
(Ps. 69:2, DRA)

Glory to the Father, and to the Son, and to the Holy Spirit: as it was in the beginning, is now, and will be forever. Amen.

Revelation 19:6-7
Hallelujah!
> For our Lord God Almighty reigns.
Let us rejoice and be glad
> and give him glory!
For the wedding of the Lamb has come,
> and his bride has made herself ready.

Intercessions
(Offer personal prayers.)

Lord's Prayer

Dismissal
O God, grant us peaceful rest with the joyful knowledge that though your kingdom is here, its magnificent fullness is still to come, through Christ Jesus, our Lord. Amen.

Personal Meditations

DAY 26 † Morning Prayer

O Lord, open my lips, and my mouth will declare your praise. (Ps. 51:15, NRSV)

Psalm 67:1-2

> May God be gracious to us and bless us
> > and make his face shine on us—
> so that your ways may be known on earth,
> > your salvation among all nations.

Glory to the Father, and to the Son, and to the Holy Spirit: as it was in the beginning, is now, and will be forever. Amen.

Hymn

> *Proclaim to every people, tongue, and nation*
> > *That God, in whom they live and move, is love.*
> *Tell how he stooped to save his lost creation*
> > *And died on earth that we might live above.*

Psalm 71:15-18

> My mouth will tell of your righteous deeds,
> > of your saving acts all day long—
> > though I know not how to relate them all.
> I will come and proclaim your mighty acts, Sovereign LORD;
> > I will proclaim your righteous deeds, yours alone.
> Since my youth, God, you have taught me,
> > and to this day I declare your marvelous deeds.
> Even when I am old and gray,
> > do not forsake me, my God,
> till I declare your power to the next generation,
> > your mighty acts to all who are to come.

Prayer

> O Lord, do not let us neglect your great gift of salvation. Instill in us a lifelong zeal to tell others of the wonderful things you have done.

Psalm 145:17-20

> The LORD is righteous in all his ways
> and faithful in all he does.
> The LORD is near to all who call on him,
> to all who call on him in truth.
> He fulfills the desires of those who fear him;
> he hears their cry and saves them.
> The LORD watches over all who love him,
> but all the wicked he will destroy.

Prayer

We love you, O God. You are just to all and ever present to save anyone who sincerely cries out to you.

Scripture Reading (Optional)   Luke 18:9-14

Reflections from Augustine

You are great, O Lord, and have "respect for the lowly, but the proud you know afar off." Nor do you draw near but to the contrite heart, nor are you found by the proud—not even if they could number by cunning skill the stars and the sand and measure the starry regions and trace the courses of the planets. (*Confessions*, 5.3.3)

(Offer personal prayers.)

The Lord's Prayer

Dismissal

Gracious Father, form us into humble vessels with hearts sensitive to your Holy Spirit. Give us a true willingness to repent when we have sinned and to seek forgiveness from you and from those whom we have wronged, through Christ Jesus, our Lord. Amen.

DAY 26 † Evening Prayer

Self-Examination

(Reflect on the day, using the following questions as a guide, confess any departures from the law of love, and ask God for forgiveness.)

- Have I become complacent and slothful in advancing my spiritual growth?
- Have I let myself become entangled in fruitless arguments over doctrine?

Opening

O God, come to my assistance; O Lord, make haste to help me.
(Ps. 69:2, DRA)

Glory to the Father, and to the Son, and to the Holy Spirit: as it was in the beginning, is now, and will be forever. Amen.

Ephesians 1:3-4

Praise be to the God and Father of our Lord Jesus Christ, who has blessed us in the heavenly realms with every spiritual blessing in Christ. For he chose us in him before the creation of the world to be holy and blameless in his sight.

Intercessions

(Offer personal prayers.)

Lord's Prayer

Dismissal

We acknowledge to you, O God, our shortcomings and ask that you bring us to the break of day strengthened with a fresh resolve and renewed zeal to live lives devoted fully to you, through your Son, Christ Jesus. Amen.

Personal Meditations

O Lord, open my lips, and my mouth will declare your praise. (Ps. 51:15, NRSV)

Psalm 67:3-4

May the peoples praise you, God;
    may all the peoples praise you.
May the nations be glad and sing for joy,
    for you rule the peoples with equity
    and guide the nations of the earth.

Glory to the Father, and to the Son, and to the Holy Spirit: as it was in the beginning, is now, and will be forever. Amen.

Hymn

Come, we that love the Lord,
    And let our joys be known;
Join in a song with sweet accord,
    And thus surround the throne.

Psalm 69:30-32

I will praise God's name in song
    and glorify him with thanksgiving.
This will please the LORD more than an ox,
    more than a bull with its horns and hooves.
The poor will see and be glad—
    you who seek God, may your hearts live!

Prayer

For delivering us from the deadly wages of sin, we adore you, O Lord. May our celebration of your mighty deeds lift the hearts of the lowly.

Psalm 73:24-26

[O God,] you guide me with your counsel,
and afterward you will take me into glory.
Whom have I in heaven but you?
And earth has nothing I desire besides you.
My flesh and my heart may fail,
but God is the strength of my heart
and my portion forever.

Prayer

O Lord, we bless your name, for whatever happens, you are always with us. Even in the face of death and ruin, you alone are our true hope and strength.

Scripture Reading (Optional)   1 John 1:5-9

Reflections from Augustine

O Fountain of Life, the only and true Creator and Ruler of the universe, by a humble piety we return to you; and you purge us from our evil habits and are merciful to the sins of those who confess to you; you "hear the groaning of the prisoner," and you release us from those fetters we have forged for ourselves, provided we do not lift up against you the willfulness of a false liberty—losing all through craving more, by loving our own private good more than you, the Good of all. (*Confessions*, 3.8.16)

(Offer personal prayers.)

The Lord's Prayer

Dismissal

We begin this day, O Merciful One, knowing that you have freed us from sin and death and bestowed on us purity and life. Help us to live purposefully with this wonderful knowledge so that we neither neglect the nurture of our souls nor the salvation of others, through Christ Jesus, our Savior and Lord. Amen.

DAY 27 † Evening Prayer

Self-Examination

(Reflect on the day, using the following questions as a guide, confess any departures from the law of love, and ask God for forgiveness.)

- Have I allowed my zeal for ministry and the salvation of others to dwindle or even disappear?
- Have I let my everyday worries strangle my hope and joy in serving Christ?

Opening

O God, come to my assistance; O Lord, make haste to help me.
(Ps. 69:2, DRA)

Glory to the Father, and to the Son, and to the Holy Spirit: as it was in the beginning, is now, and will be forever. Amen.

Ephesians 1:7-8

In [Christ] we have redemption through his blood, the forgiveness of sins, in accordance with the riches of God's grace that he lavished on us.

Intercessions

(Offer personal prayers.)

Lord's Prayer

Dismissal

We end our day rejoicing and praising you, O God, for our fears are banished and our worries dispelled at the knowledge of our great salvation purchased by the blood of your Son, in whose name we pray. Amen.

Personal Meditations

DAY 28 † Morning Prayer

O Lord, open my lips, and my mouth will declare your praise. (Ps. 51:15, NRSV)

Psalm 67:5-7

May the peoples praise you, God;
　　may all the peoples praise you.
The land yields its harvest;
　　God, our God, blesses us.
May God bless us still,
　　so that all the ends of the earth will fear him.

Glory to the Father, and to the Son, and to the Holy Spirit: as it was in the beginning, is now, and will be forever. Amen.

Hymn

He leadeth me! O blessed thought!
　　O words with heavenly comfort fraught!
Whate'er I do, where'er I be,
　　Still 'tis God's hand that leadeth me.

Psalm 23:1-4

The LORD is my shepherd, I lack nothing.
　　He makes me lie down in green pastures,
he leads me beside quiet waters,
　　he refreshes my soul.
He guides me along the right paths
　　for his name's sake.
Even though I walk
　　through the darkest valley,
I will fear no evil,
　　for you are with me;
your rod and your staff,
　　they comfort me.

Prayer

O Shepherd of our souls, we put our trust in you. You guide us to havens of rest and renewal, and you comfort us when times are bleak.

Psalm 27:4-5

One thing I ask from the LORD,
    this only do I seek:
that I may dwell in the house of the LORD
    all the days of my life,
to gaze on the beauty of the LORD
    and to seek him in his temple.
For in the day of trouble
    he will keep me safe in his dwelling;
he will hide me in the shelter of his sacred tent
    and set me high upon a rock.

Prayer

We rejoice, O divine Master, for you alone are the Surety of our lives; you are our Hope and Support. May we always find refuge with you.

Scripture Reading (Optional)   Romans 14:8-9

Reflections from Augustine

If we have received the grace of regeneration, death shall not injure us, even if we should forthwith depart from this life; "for to this end Christ both died, and rose, and revived, that he might be Lord both of the dead and the living"; nor shall death retain dominion over us for whom Christ freely died. (*Enchiridion*, chap. 120)

(Offer personal prayers.)

The Lord's Prayer

Dismissal

O gracious God, at great cost you have freed us from the scourge of death and granted us new life. We belong to you. Help us to serve you by doing good works and telling others the good news of Christ, in whose name we pray. Amen.

DAY 28 † Evening Prayer

Self-Examination

(Reflect on the day, using the following questions as a guide, confess any departures from the law of love, and ask God for forgiveness.)

- Have I compromised my Christian standards for occupational success or social acceptance?
- Have I let my reliance on money and the pursuit of financial security inhibit me from depending on God and living a life of risky obedience to him?

Opening

O God, come to my assistance; O Lord, make haste to help me.
(Ps. 69:2, DRA)

Glory to the Father, and to the Son, and to the Holy Spirit: as it was in the beginning, is now, and will be forever. Amen.

Colossians 1:12-14

[Give] joyful thanks to the Father, who has qualified you to share in the inheritance of his holy people in the kingdom of light. For he has rescued us from the dominion of darkness and brought us into the kingdom of the Son he loves, in whom we have redemption, the forgiveness of sins.

Intercessions

(Offer personal prayers.)

Lord's Prayer

Dismissal

O God, because you have delivered us from the darkness of sin, we find rest and peace, though the shadows of night surround us, through Christ Jesus, our Lord. Amen.

Personal Meditations

DAY 29 † Morning Prayer

O Lord, open my lips, and my mouth will declare your praise. (Ps. 51:15, NRSV)

Psalm 24:1-2

The earth is the LORD's, and everything in it,
 the world, and all who live in it;
for he founded it on the seas
 and established it on the waters.

Glory to the Father, and to the Son, and to the Holy Spirit: as it was in the beginning, is now, and will be forever. Amen.

Hymn

Glory be to God above,
 God from whom all blessings flow;
Make we mention of his love,
 Publish we his praise below.

Psalm 96:1-3

Sing to the LORD a new song;
 sing to the LORD, all the earth.
Sing to the LORD, praise his name;
 proclaim his salvation day after day.
Declare his glory among the nations,
 his marvelous deeds among all peoples.

Prayer

Blessed are you, O Lord, our God, for your great salvation. All the nations of the world will take notice and praise your name.

Psalm 34:1-5

I will extol the LORD at all times;
> his praise will always be on my lips.
I will glory in the LORD;
> let the afflicted hear and rejoice.
Glorify the LORD with me;
> let us exalt his name together.
I sought the LORD, and he answered me;
> he delivered me from all my fears.
Those who look to him are radiant;
> their faces are never covered with shame.

Prayer

O God, we rejoice exceedingly and lift our hearts in adoration to you, for through the sacrifice of your Son you have rescued us from fear and destruction.

Scripture Reading (Optional)   1 Peter 1:3-9

Reflections from Augustine

Let it be far, O Lord—let it be far from the heart of your servant who confesses to you; let it be far from me to think myself happy from just any kind of joy. For there is a joy that is not granted to the wicked but to those who worship you thankfully, whose joy you yourself are. And the happy life is this—to rejoice unto you, in you, and for you; this it is, and there is no other. But those who think there is another follow after another joy, which is not the true one. (*Confessions*, 10.22.32)

(Offer personal prayers.)

The Lord's Prayer

Dismissal

We are filled with great joy, O Father, because of the surpassing love you have shown to us. Help us to share that joy with other people by being bearers of your love to them, through your Son, Christ Jesus. Amen.

DAY 29 † Evening Prayer

Self-Examination

(Reflect on the day, using the following questions as a guide, confess any departures from the law of love, and ask God for forgiveness.)

- Have I actively pursued spiritual growth by making such disciplines as prayer, Scripture reading, and fasting a daily part of my life?
- Have I participated in the sacrament of Eucharist as often as I have opportunity?

Opening

O God, come to my assistance; O Lord, make haste to help me.
(Ps. 69:2, DRA)

Glory to the Father, and to the Son, and to the Holy Spirit: as it was in the beginning, is now, and will be forever. Amen.

Colossians 1:15-16

The Son is the image of the invisible God, the firstborn over all creation. For in him all things were created: things in heaven and on earth, visible and invisible, whether thrones or powers or rulers or authorities; all things have been created through him and for him.

Intercessions

(Offer personal prayers.)

Lord's Prayer

Dismissal

Our hearts are at rest, O Holy One, knowing that even as we sleep, you watch over the world we live in and hold all creation together, through Christ Jesus, our Lord. Amen.

Personal Meditations

DAY 30 † Morning Prayer

O Lord, open my lips, and my mouth will declare your praise. (Ps. 51:15, NRSV)

Psalm 24:3-5

Who may ascend the mountain of the LORD?
>Who may stand in his holy place?
The one who has clean hands and a pure heart,
>who does not trust in an idol
>or swear by a false god.
They will receive blessing from the LORD
>and vindication from God their Savior.

Glory to the Father, and to the Son, and to the Holy Spirit: as it was in the beginning, is now, and will be forever. Amen.

Hymn

There's a wideness in God's mercy,
>*Like the wideness of the sea;*
There's a kindness in his justice,
>*Which is more than liberty.*

Psalm 80:1-3

Hear us, Shepherd of Israel,
>you who lead Joseph like a flock.
You who sit enthroned between the cherubim,
>shine forth before Ephraim, Benjamin and Manasseh.
Awaken your might;
>come and save us.
Restore us, O God;
>make your face shine on us,
>that we may be saved.

Prayer

We adore you, O loving Shepherd, because you have looked on us,
responding to our need, and blessed us with your abundant grace. We
exalt you, O Savior of our souls.

Psalm 77:13-15

Your ways, God, are holy.
> What god is as great as our God?
You are the God who performs miracles;
> you display your power among the peoples.
With your mighty arm you redeemed your people,
> the descendants of Jacob and Joseph.

Prayer

O God, may our lives reflect the mighty work of deliverance you have
performed for us. Through your Son, Christ Jesus, the God-man, you
have reconciled us to yourself.

Scripture Reading (Optional)   1 Timothy 2:1-6

Reflections from Augustine

We could not be redeemed, even through the one Mediator between God
and humanity, the man Christ Jesus, if he were not also God. Now when
Adam was created, he, being a righteous man, had no need of a mediator.
But when sin had placed a wide gulf between God and the human race,
it was expedient that a Mediator, who alone of the human race was born,
lived, and died without sin, should reconcile us to God, and procure
even for our bodies a resurrection to eternal life, in order that the pride
of humanity might be exposed and cured through the humility of God.
(*Enchiridion*, chap. 108)

(Offer personal prayers.)

The Lord's Prayer

Dismissal

O Father, having reconciled us to yourself through your Son, Jesus, and
filled us with joy, sustain our devotion to you through the power of your
Holy Spirit. In the name of that same Son, Christ Jesus, we pray. Amen.

DAY 30 † Evening Prayer

Self-Examination

(Reflect on the day, using the following questions as a guide, confess any departures from the law of love, and ask God for forgiveness.)

- Have I failed to elevate loving God and my neighbor over the possession or practice of any spiritual gift or ministry?
- Have I submitted myself to God in every way so that his love completely governs my intentions, words, and deeds?

Opening

O God, come to my assistance; O Lord, make haste to help me.
(Ps. 69:2, DRA)

Glory to the Father, and to the Son, and to the Holy Spirit: as it was in the beginning, is now, and will be forever. Amen.

Colossians 1:17-18

[Christ] is before all things, and in him all things hold together. And he is the head of the body, the church; he is the beginning and the firstborn from among the dead, so that in everything he might have the supremacy.

Intercessions

(Offer personal prayers.)

Lord's Prayer

Dismissal

O holy Christ, you are our gracious and merciful Master. Grant that this night and every night we may rest with the assurance that your love governs all. In your name, O Lord, we pray. Amen.

Personal Meditations

Sources

Augustine. *The City of God*. In *Nicene and Post-Nicene Fathers, First Series*. Edited by Philip Schaff. 1886. Reprint, Peabody, MA: Hendrickson Publishers, 1994, 2:1-511.

―――. "Concerning Faith of Things Not Seen." In Schaff, *Nicene and Post-Nicene Fathers*, 3:337-43.

―――. *The Confessions*. In Schaff, *Nicene and Post-Nicene Fathers*, 1:45-207.

―――. *The Enchiridion*. In Schaff, *Nicene and Post-Nicene Fathers*, 3:237-76.

―――. *On the Gospel of St. John*. In Schaff, *Nicene and Post-Nicene Fathers*, 7:7-452.

―――. *Soliloquies*. In Schaff, *Nicene and Post-Nicene Fathers*, 7:538-60.

Bible, Ken, comp. *Wesley Hymns*. Kansas City: Lillenas Publishing, 1982. Hymns adapted from this source are listed as follows by day (boldface), hymn number, and author/translator: **4**, 82, C. Wesley; **18**, 70, Lange/J. Wesley; **20**, 16, C. Wesley; **24**, 143, C. Wesley; **29**, 101, C. Wesley.

Book of Common Prayer (BCP). New York: Church Hymnal Corporation, 1979. The psalm selections in most cases follow the order of the Daily Office Lectionary in the BCP, beginning with Proper 9.

Hymnary.org. http://www.hymnary.org/texts?qu=+in:texts. Most hymns used are also on this site. The *Hymnary* version of the hymn for Day 21 was used instead of the *Sing to the Lord* version (no. 64).

Sing to the Lord. Kansas City: Lillenas Publishing, 1993. Hymns adapted from this source are listed as follows by day (boldface), hymn number, and author/translator: **1**, 54, Montgomery; **2**, 51, Robinson; **3**, 52 (v. 2), Schütz/Cox; **5**, 30, Luther/Hedge; **6**, 548, Bonar; **7**, 42, Lyte; **8**, 55, Brooke; **9**, 303, Watts; **10**, 36, Crosby; **11**, 464, C. Wesley; **12**, 473, Crosby; **13**, 147, C. Wesley; **14**, 429, Bliss; **15**, 59, Plumptre; **16**, 490, Chisholm; **17**, 698, Nichol; **19**, 16, Bonar; **22**, 12, Franz/Walworth; **23**, 21, anonymous; **25**, 52 (v. 1), Schütz/Cox; **26**, 712, Thomson; **27**, 18, Watts; **28**, 99, Gilmore; **30**, 81, Faber.